THE SESAME STREET
TREASURY

Featuring Jim Henson's Sesame Street Muppets

VOLUME 8

STARRING
THE NUMBER
8
AND THE LETTERS
K AND L

Children's Television Workshop/Funk & Wagnalls, Inc.

WRITTEN BY:
Linda Bove with the National Theatre of the Deaf
Michael Frith
Linda Hayward
Emily Perl Kingsley
Sharon Lerner
Jeffrey Moss
Norman Stiles
Pat Tornborg
Daniel Wilcox

ILLUSTRATED BY:
Rick Brown
Tom Cooke
Robert Dennis
Mary Grace Eubank
Michael Frith
Joe Mathieu
Marc Nadel
Michael J. Smollin
Maggie Swanson
Kay Wood

PHOTOGRAPHS BY:
John E. Barrett
Charles Rowan
Neil Selkirk
View-Master International Group

Here come the **K**s!

A Silly **K** Poem

A **kangaroo** named **Kathy**
Came hopping into town.
She brought along her **kid**
Whom she dressed up all in brown.
She **kept** him in her pocket,
Which she locked up with a **key,**
But every night she took him out
And **kissed** him 1, 2, 3.

Grover's Little Kitten

GREETINGS! I AM THE COUNT. DO YOU KNOW WHY I AM CALLED THE COUNT? BECAUSE I LOVE TO *COUNT*— ANYTHING! MY VERY FAVORITE RECIPE IS THIS LUNCHTIME LOG THAT IS MADE UP OF TWENTY SEPARATE LITTLE PIECES, AND I COUNT *EACH ONE* AS I MAKE IT!

1, 2, 3. THAT'S ENOUGH FOR ME.
4, 5, 6. HOW MANY SHALL I FIX?
7, 8, 9. I'LL INVITE MY UNCLE AND COUSIN.
ADD 10, 11, AND 12 – AND THAT'S AN EVEN DOZEN.

13, 14, AND 15, IN CASE THERE'S AN EXTRA GUEST.
16, 17, 18 WILL SURELY FEED THE REST.
BUT I WANT TO GO ON COUNTING, SO I'LL ADD 19 AND 20.
I DON'T KNOW *HOW* MANY I'LL FEED, BUT I'LL COUNT ON HAVING *PLENTY!*

THE COUNT'S TWENTY-IS-PLENTY LOG

To serve four or five—
What you need:
1 loaf of snack-sized dark pumpernickel bread
2 3-ounce packages of cream cheese
⅓ cup of orange juice
⅓ cup of chopped nuts (any kind)

What you do:
Let the cream cheese soften before starting. Put the soft cream cheese in a bowl, and pour in the orange juice. Mix them with a wooden spoon until they are as creamy as mayonnaise. Then stir in the chopped nuts.

Count 20 slices of bread, and spread them with cheese. Then make little stacks of bread and cheese. Say the Count's poem as you work. When you've finished stacking, tip each stack onto its side, and push all the stacks end-to-end. They should stick together like a long log. Frost the log with what's left of the cheese, and put it in the freezer for an hour. Have a grownup help you slice the log diagonally.

K k

The Pied Kazoo-er of Kamlin

Once upon a time, there was a town named Kamlin. And Kamlin had a problem. Kamlin had too many kangaroos.

Kamlin had kangaroos everywhere. Kangaroos in the kitchens. Kangaroos in the kindergarten. Kangaroos in the keyholes. Uptown, downtown, and midtown, there were kangaroos, kangaroos, kangaroos!

The townspeople couldn't stand it. So they had a town meeting. Mayor Kinkaid made a speech. She said, "We've got too many kangaroos!" And everybody cheered.

Then she said, "We need a plan!" And everybody stopped cheering. Because nobody had a plan. So they all sat there, thinking very hard.

Then up walked a keen-eyed stranger. He was dressed from head to foot in patchwork, and under his arm he carried a long kazoo.

"My friends," he said, "I am the Pied Kazoo-er, and I have the key to your kangaroo problem."

"Are you kidding?" said a townsperson. "How can you solve our kangaroo problem? By playing your kazoo?"

"Yes," said the Pied Kazoo-er, smiling mysteriously, and he raised his kazoo to his lips. Instantly, the air was filled with strange and enchanting music.

Then something magical happened. As the Pied Kazoo-er walked along, playing his kazoo, people began to follow him. All the people on King Street followed him. All the people on Kite Hill followed him. All the people who heard his bewitching music followed him.

In fact, all the people in the whole town of Kamlin followed him. They followed him out of Kamlin to a kingdom far away, where they never saw another kangaroo again.

When the people left, the kangaroos took over the town of Kamlin. They made it a kangaroo town. It became busy and prosperous, and soon it was the biggest, most famous kangaroo town in the world.

And the kangaroos lived happily ever after. So did the people.

And, by the way, just in case you didn't notice: Kamlin, and kangaroo, and kazoo . . . and lots of other words in this story, too . . . all start with the letter K. It's true. See for yourself.

The Count

Home: The Castle, Transylvania

Favorite Food: Birthday cake with lots of candles

Best Friend: Countess Dahling Von Dahling

Pets: Bats and Fatatita the Cat

Favorite Activity: Counting stars in the sky, grains of sand on the beach, Big Bird's feathers, etc.

Favorite Stories: "Three Little Pigs," "Goldilocks and the Three Bears," "Snow White and the Seven Dwarfs"

Favorite Way to Fall Asleep: Counting sheep

Favorite Saying: "You can count on me!"

LA COCINA DE COOKIE MONSTER
COOKIE MONSTER'S KITCHEN

Say it in Spanish!

fregadero
sink

refrigerador
refrigerator

hornilla
stove

rodillo
rolling pin

mesa
table

molde
cookie cutter

maggie

tetera
teakettle

plato
plate

tenedor
fork

olla
pot

taza
cup

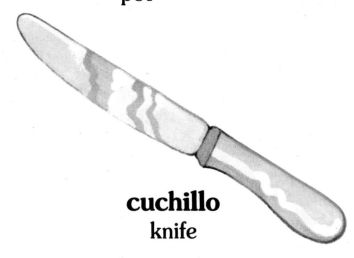

cuchillo
knife

L¹

The Legend of Lasso Louise

This is Frazzle. Today is his birthday. His aunt Frazzie brought him a surprise—two scrumptious, whirligig pops. The blue one is Frazzle's favorite flavor, blueberry-tangerine-vanilla. The other pop is tangerine-vanilla-raspberry mint. But two pops are too many, even for a great big monster like Frazzle. Which one would you like?

action

Action Words

jump

walk

run

climb

stand

sit

kneel

How many things in this picture can you "sign"?

very

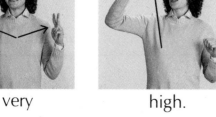
high.

Cookie and the Count LOVE the Baker

Long, long ago, in a lavish lodge near the village of
Liverwurst, lived a lovely lass called Linda the Lonely.
Linda was lonely because, ever since she was a little
girl, she had been locked in the lodge by her wicked
uncle, Lord Ludwig of Liverwurst.

"Alas, alack. What a lousy life I live!" lamented Linda.
"Let me loose! Let me loose!"

But Lord Ludwig laughed loudly. "Not likely, my little
lamb! I still have loads and loads of work for you to do!"

For long hours Linda labored in Lord Ludwig's library, lifting lots and lots of books. Every day Lord Ludwig would yell, "Linda, you lunk, stop loafing! Where is my lunch? It is late."

Linda lugged Lord Ludwig's large lunch from the larder.

"What have you brought me, you little lump?" asked Lord Ludwig as Linda ladled out his luscious lunch of leafy lettuce, large lobsters, lovely lentils, lima beans, leg of lamb, licorice, lollipops and lemonade.

"Oh, Uncle Ludwig!" Linda lamented, "I have been laboring long hours on your library ladder! Please let me have a little lunch, too."

"Later, lazybones . . . if there's any lunch left! Ha, ha! Now leave— and get back to your ladder!"

Late one night, in the loft where she lived, Linda laid her lonely head upon her lumpy little bed. Suddenly she heard voices. Linda leaned out the window to listen.

Lord Ludwig and a lanky lad were on the lawn. "I know I am late with your laundry, Lord Ludwig," said the lad. "But there is so little light and it is such a *large* load of laundry."

"None of your lip, lout! Get a lamp if there is no light—but lather up that laundry or there will be lots of lashes where you least like 'em!"

With that, Lord Ludwig left.

Linda took a lantern and leaned out of the window. She leapt onto the limb of a lemon tree, and lowered herself lightly onto the lawn.

"Who are you?" asked the lanky lad.

"I am Lord Ludwig's niece, Linda the Lonely. Who are you?"

"I am Lloyd of London, Lord Ludwig's lowliest lackey. And I am lonely, too."

"Listen, Lloyd," lilted Linda. "I have long longed to leave this loathsome lodge. Let me tell you my plan! Listen..."

"La," laughed Lloyd. "It's so loony, it just might work!"

Late the next day, Lloyd lugged his load of laundry
into Lord Ludwig's library. "Look, Linda," said Lloyd
as he lifted his lute from under Ludwig's lavender
leggings. "I have brought my lute."

"It's lovely, Lloyd. Now lend me your long leather
laces so I can make a lasso."

Linda told Lloyd
to lull Lord Ludwig
with a lilting
lullaby on his lute.
Soon Lord Ludwig
was fast asleep.

Like lightning, Linda looped her lasso around Lord Ludwig's legs and lashed him to the library ladder.

"Help!" yelled Lord Ludwig. "I want to call my lawyer."

"You'll have lots of time for that, you lily-livered lizard! You're going to learn your lesson. You'll be locked up for a long, long time, laboring in the laundry of the local jail!"

Linda lifted a large key from Ludwig's leather belt, unlocked the lodge's locks and lifted the latch.

"Now, Lloyd, let's leave!" laughed Linda.

"Linda," said Lloyd, "it was a lucky day for me when you leapt from that lemon tree."

"Then we shall call you Lloyd the Lucky," said Linda.

"And you shall be Linda the Lionhearted," said Lloyd.

"And," they said together, "we won't be lonely any longer."

The Lemonade Stand

Oh look!
A lemonade stand.
Everybody bringing
something to help.
Ernie bring sugar.
Count bring 12 lemons
(he counted them).
Bert bring pitcher
of ice water.
Isabella make sign.
That is COOPERATION.
Now guess who help
MIX lemonade...

GULP!

YUM!

OH BOY!

That was very
good lemonade.
And that pitcher
was DELICIOUS!
Sign not bad,
either.
Thanks.

Ernie and Bert's Counting Story

4 books

Wait till you see what I've found now, Bert!

5 jack-in-the-boxes

6 Tyrolean hats

7 airplanes

8 saddle shoes

Knock Knock

Ernie is trying to find his friend's house.
Can you help him?
Ernie's friend's house is blue.
Touch the houses that are blue.
Ernie's friend's house has a yellow door.
Touch the blue houses that have yellow doors.
Ernie's friend's house has a flower in the window.
Touch the blue houses with the yellow doors that have flowers in the windows.
Ernie's friend's house has a cat on the roof.
Touch Ernie's friend's house.

OLD KING COLE

Old King Cole
Was a merry old soul,
   And a merry old soul was he;

He called for his pipe,
And he called for his bowl,
   And he called for his fiddlers three!

A B C

F G H

L M N O

S T U

Y Z 1 2

6 7